A Microsoft® P

MULTIMEDIA MANAGER
INSTRUCTOR'S RESOURCE CD

for

HISTORY

For Spielvogel's
Western Civilization, Sixth Edition

THOMSON
—————— TM
WADSWORTH

Australia • Brazil • Canada • Mexico
Singapore • Spain • United Kingdom • United States

Thomson Higher Education
10 Davis Drive
Belmont, CA 94002-3098
USA

TABLE OF CONTENTS

POWERPOINT GUIDE

POWERPOINT GUIDE
Larry J. Steck
Lake Michigan College

I. Introduction

A. **Purpose:** This booklet is intended primarily for the user who is unfamiliar with PowerPoint as a presentation tool. PowerPoint is an easy tool to begin using in the classroom. However its ease of use can be deceptive. The more you use it, the more things you will discover you can do. There are excellent books on the market for those already familiar with the basics. For those who are not, what follows should be of some assistance.

B. **Scope:** There are four major components to this booklet. The first section will help you navigate through the accompanying Multimedia Manager CD as it comes from the publisher. An experienced educator has developed the CD, and you may well find that it works for you as produced. However, should you wish to modify the CD presentations, you may do so rather easily. This booklet's second section will take you through some of the basics of creating your own PowerPoint presentation. Once you have learned these techniques, the third section will allow you to employ them. It will guide you through the process of transferring a presentation on the MM CD to your own computer's hard drive, modifying that presentation to suit your needs, and suggesting how you may best save your final product for classroom use. Finally, section four will discuss several ways in which you may give students access to your presentations.

C. **Understanding the Shorthand Directions:** Navigating through your MM CD and using PowerPoint either to make a new presentation or to modify an existing one is not difficult, but it does require some modest assistance. The guidance in this booklet is written specifically for a PC-style computer running PowerPoint 2000. The MM CD accompanying the booklet has been field-tested on a PC running PowerPoint 2000, also using PowerPoint 97, and on a MAC running PowerPoint 98 and 2001. Navigation on a Mac is somewhat different from PC navigation, but using PowerPoint is rather similar in all four versions. The directions for one version are quickly adaptable to the others. Below is a list of navigation abbreviations used throughout this booklet to guide you (acronyms are no fun but they do save space).

click	= one click with the left mouse button
dc	= double click left button
drag and drop	= with this symbol ⊕ showing in a highlighted box, hold down the left mouse button and with your cursor move the object/slide to its new location, then release the button
highlight	= hold down the left mouse button and drag the cursor across the desired text and release the button
PPT	= PowerPoint 2000
rc	= right click
resize	= with your text or graphics inside a box, put your cursor on one of the clear corner boxes, hold down the left mouse button and move the cursor to enlarge or reduce; moving the middle squares will distort the graphic.
→	= go to the next step (it will open automatically or by one left click)

II. Using the MM CD Without Modification

A. Getting Started with Your MM CD

1. Turn on your computer and make sure that the sound is on for both the computer and your speakers.

2. Insert the MM CD in the CD-ROM drive.

3. → Start → Programs → PPT → PPT Starting Dialog Box (below).

STARTING DIALOG BOX

4. Make sure the "Open an existing presentation" circle has the black dot and click OK.

5. Your next screen is the OPEN screen (see below).

OPEN SCREEN

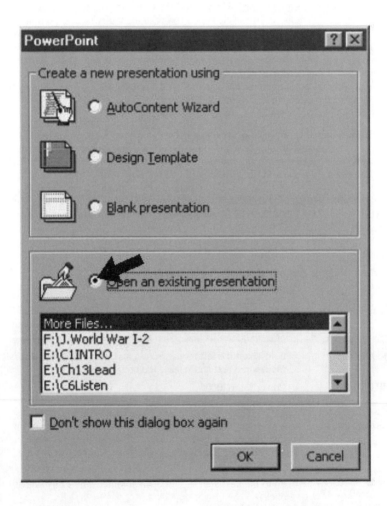

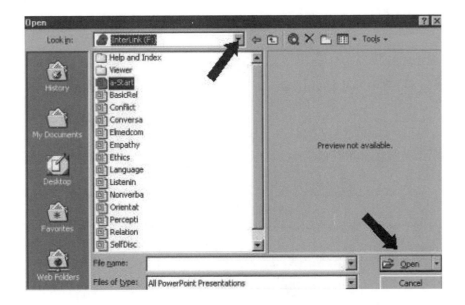

6. Click the Down Arrow in the **LOOK IN** box then find and click on (highlight) the CD-ROM drive letter in that box. A screen similar to the one above will appear. To access the contents of your MM CD, click on (highlight) the desired presentation title, then click on the **OPEN** box.

   Note: On the MM CD used for this booklet there are files other than PPT files on the disk. Their icons look like manila file folders. These other files include an electronic copy of this guide plus indices of the CNN videos, movies, text chapters, and PPT slides on the MM CD. The Viewer Folder contains a PPT viewer for your use should your classroom computer not have PPT installed. Some MM CDs also have a START PPT presentation that contains the CD credits, a Table of Contents, and a hot button for our Web site.

7. Once you have selected a PPT presentation to view and clicked the **OPEN** box, your show will load automatically. However it may take a few moments—particularly if it contains a video, which takes a lot of computer memory. Be patient and wait until the presentation is fully loaded on your computer before going to the next step.

8. To play your presentation from this first screen → Slide Show → View Show on the Main Menu (see the figure on the following page) or press the **F5** key on your keyboard.

9. Each mouse click hereafter will move you one more step in the PPT presentation, either to a new view on the same slide or to a new slide, until you reach the final (blank) slide.

10. At this blank ending slide, either click on the triangle in the lower left corner of the slide (see next page) or press the **ESC** key, which will end the presentation and return you to the Slide Sorter View.

3

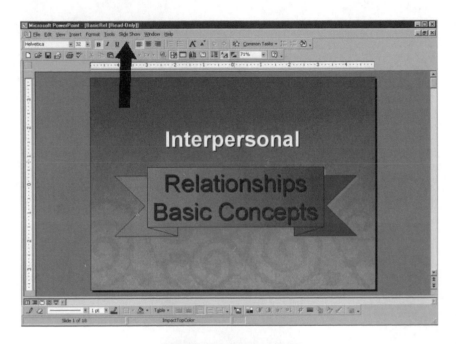

B. Instructional Advice for Using Your MM CD

1. **PRACTICE, PRACTICE, PRACTICE.** An experienced college professor prepared these PPT presentations on the basis of the accompany text and has field-tested them in the classroom. It is advisable to view the slide show prior to presentation to review the slides' sequence, contents, and animation. You will note that animation of some slides is automatic, while on others you will need a mouse click to trigger the next item. Prior practice and/or printing your slides will acquaint you with the details of a show and thus produce a smooth presentation.

2. **PATIENCE.** Heavily animated graphic files and video clips require a lot of computer memory, and there may be a pause on your screen while a slide loads. On early versions of the MM CDs, movie clips will run automatically a few seconds after their initial appearance, while on a Mac you have to click on the movie to start it. On later versions of the MM CDs they will run automatically on both platforms.

3. When a video clip has finished playing, click on the frame around the movie, not on the movie, to move to the next slide.

4

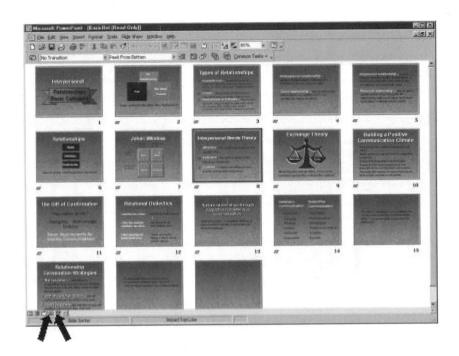

4. If you wish to start your presentation with a slide other than the first slide in a given presentation, you may do so by using Slide Sorter. When the first slide in the presentation appears, click on the **Slide Sorter View** button in the lower left of your window. This view allows you to see all slides in the selected show. Click on the slide you wish to appear first (a solid blue line appears around the edge of the slide). Now click on the Slide Show button immediately to the right of the Slide Sorter View button, and your show will start with the designated slide.

III. Creating Your Own PPT Presentation

This section introduces you to basic techniques for making your own PPT presentation and will give you some basics on how you may modify and personalize your MM CD.

A. Choosing a Template

The fastest, most effective way to put together a PPT presentation is to take advantage of templates and customize them to suit your needs. Templates are artistic blueprints that provide preformatted, professionally designed backgrounds, images, bullets, and text colors and sizes that make for readable, eye-catching slides. These templates can also be altered to suit your needs if you prefer other options.

1. Selecting and applying a template to a presentation begins by opening the PPT Program. At the Starting Dialog Box select the **Design Template** option and click Open. The next screen allows you to see thumbnail previews of the template choices. Click on each template title to see a preview of what it looks like, and when you have found what you want, click OK to select your preferred design.

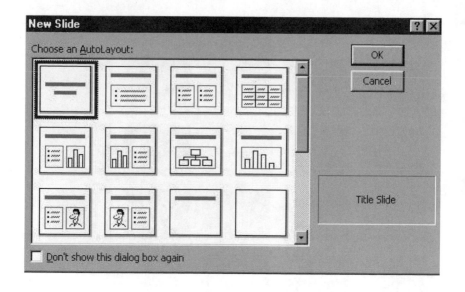

2. The next window is the **New Slide AutoLayout**. Here you choose from one of 24 layouts (12 visible) for the kind of slide you will need. The first and next-to-last visible choices are for title or introductory slides. The remaining choices are for slides with text, graphs, graphics, or video in different arrangements. Make your choice and click OK. PPT will automatically take you to a status called **Normal View**. Once in this status, you will be able to add text, images, sound, and/or motion to a slide.

Note: As you are constructing your presentation you may decide that you prefer to use a template design other than the first one you chose. You may select another design template but realize that the new design will be applied to all of your slides in that PPT presentation. PPT does not allow you to mix and match within a presentation. Also, changing templates may change the style of print and the spacing of words on the slides already created. Some backtracking and editing may be needed. If you wish, you may also delete the template background graphics from a slide by → Format → Background. Click on the "Omit background . . ." box and then click on Apply.

B. Adding Text to Your Slide

There are three ways to add text to a slide.

1. Each new slide you create reserves a partitioned zone where you can type your text (except for instances when you choose to create a completely blank slide). These "type here" zones are called **text boxes**. Notice that the placeholders **Click to add title** and **Click to add text** occupy the text boxes until you click and replace them with your own text.

2. Text may also be added by inserting a text box. You may add as many text boxes to any slide as you like. Each text box can be formatted and moved independently from all other text boxes. To add a text box, on the PPT Menu Bar → Insert → Text Box, then move your cursor to the slide and click. You may now begin typing your text in the activated box.

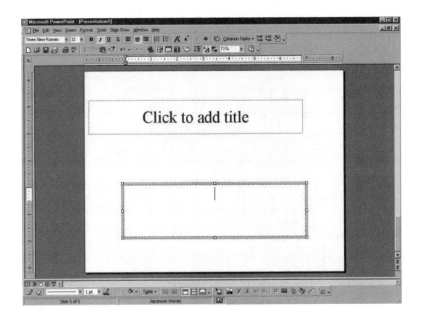

3. You may also import text into a text box from another program such as a word processing program. Use the copy feature of your word processing program to copy the desired text. Return to your PPT slide, go to the Main Menu Bar → Insert → Text Box → click on your slide to create the box then → Edit → Paste and click.

4. Once you have entered your text, you may reposition it by clicking on the text to activate the text box border. Move your cursor to this border and when this symbol ✛ appears, drag and drop the box to its new location.

5. To alter the size or style of your text, make sure your PPT Formatting Toolbar (below) is active (visible). If it is not active, then activate it: → View → Toolbar → Formatting then click. You will now see a toolbar that includes a pull-down window on the left that lists a wide variety of print styles (New Times Roman and Arial are two styles stable on both a PC and Mac). Once you have chosen your style, you may select the size of your letters by using the next pull-down box (for slide titles consider a font size of at least 40 and for the remainder of the text 28).

Note: You may also resize your text using the A A symbols. Highlight the text you wish to resize, then click on the symbol to change the font size. On this same toolbar, B represents bold, I italics, U underline, and the next 3 buttons will register your text right, center, or left. To apply, simply highlight the desired text, then click on the appropriate symbol and click a second time off the symbol.

6. The design template you selected automatically chose your text color. But you may change it if you wish. To do so make sure your **Drawing Toolbar** is active (→ View → Toolbar → Drawing). Highlight the text whose color you wish to change, then

click on the Drawing Toolbar **down triangle** symbol next to the **A** with a bar below it. This will give you a pop-up window with several added color choices, and if you want even more choices, just click at the spot offering **More Colors**. Upon selecting the desired color, go back to the highlighted text on your slide and click off the highlighted area to apply the color. Or, you can right click and go to Font, which will allow you to change color, size, etc.

C. Adding Images to Your Slide

1. There are two types of images that can be imported into a PPT presentation: clip art and photographs. Clip art is drawn images, like cartoons, made up of lines and sometimes color. Photographs are composed of rows and columns of colored dots called pixels.

2. You may add images from the PPT Clip Art Gallery to your slides by moving to the slide where you want to add an image: on the Standard Toolbar → Insert → Picture → Clip Art → Picture or Motion Clip → the image category you desire from those provided on the Insert ClipArt pop-up window (see below), and click on your category.

3. Scroll through the images in that category until you locate one you want. To place it in your slide, click on the image you want and then click on the top (Insert) icon in the pop-up box that appears. To preview before insertion, click on the second icon from the top.

4. Now you may resize, reposition, or delete the inserted image.

    To resize the image, place your cursor on one of the white boxes located at the corners of the image, hold down your mouse button and then move the edges of the image to enlarge or reduce its size.

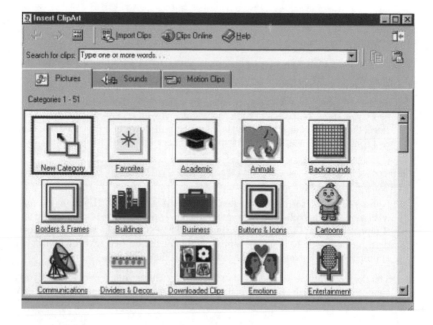

To move the image around your slide, click on the image, hold down the mouse button and move the image where you want it.

If you are not happy with the image that you have inserted, **delete** the image by clicking on the image and then pressing the Delete key. If you realize that deleting the image was a mistake, → Edit → Undo Clear or go to the Undo button (left bending arrow) on the Standard Toolbar.

5. Adding images from other sources

You can import images from the Internet, from photo CDs, from CDs of clip art, from scanners—the sources are endless. Remember that photographs from some sources are copyrighted and may require a licensing fee or royalty for use. Also it is proper form to cite your source on the slide upon which you place your inserted image.

To insert an image from an outside source, it must be in a format that PPT will accept. There are over 20 such formats, some of the more commonly used being:

BMP:	Bitmap; a Windows format
EPS:	Encapsulated PostScript; used by drawing programs
GIF:	Graphics Interchange Format; common on the Internet
JPG:	Joint Photographics Expert Group format: common on the Internet
PCD:	Kodak Photo CD format
PCT or PICT:	a standard Macintosh format
TIF:	Tag Image File Format: the cross-platform format of choice

To insert an image from the Internet launch your Internet browser, navigate to the site and image you wish to place in your presentation and then rc on the image you want to copy. Click on Copy in the pop-up window. Close or minimize the browser window and navigate to the appropriate PPT slide. The process will be quicker if you have your PPT presentation open but minimized before you go to the Internet. Then once you have captured the image from the Internet all you will have to do is maximize the PPT and complete the insertion process. To insert → Edit → Paste. You may now resize, reposition, or delete using the standard method. Cite your source under or next to your clip.

To insert an image from a CD, Zip, or floppy with a format compatible with PPT, first go to the PPT slide where you want to add the image then → Insert → Picture (From File → the disk drive on which the image files are located (A, C, D, etc.) → the image file you want to insert. Another method of capture available is Alt+Print Screen. This will copy your entire active window onto the clipboard. You may now go to your PPT slide and → Edit → Paste.

D. Adding Sounds

1. Adding music, sound effects, and other audio clips to your PPT slides adds a third, exciting dimension to your lecture. PPT comes with a library of audio files—but beware: audio can take up a lot of disk space on your hard drive. Each second of sound takes around 10K or more of space. Use sound to embellish your lecture; don't use it as a substitute for lecturing.

2. Inserting audio into a PPT presentation is as simple as making your choice and pasting that choice onto a slide.

3. One type of sound you may use is coordinated with the appearance of visual materials on your slide. To employ this sound; with the desired PPT slide in the Normal View → Slide Show → Custom Animation → Effects → highlight the desired sound → OK and click.

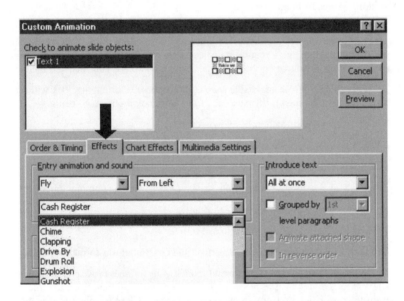

4. A second set of sounds is found in the PPT Sound Gallery (see the next figure). To access these → Insert → Movies and Sounds → Sound from Gallery → when the Insert Sound window appears, select your category and then your choice of sound or music from among the options offered. Once you have clicked on the chosen sound, you will be asked if you want it to play automatically when the slide appears or activate it with a mouse click. After making your choice, PPT returns you to the Normal View, where you will see a megaphone symbol for your sound. Reposition and resize it as needed. Note that gallery sounds only function if the computer on which you play your presentation has the designated sound in its Sound Gallery.

5. You may also import sounds and music from other sources just as you import images. Just like images, audio clips must be in a file format that is recognized by PPT. Two of the more popular are waveform files (*.WAV) and Musical Instrument Digital Interface, or MIDI files (*.MID). With the right equipment you may also insert your own recorded narration or any other sounds you might wish to copy. More advanced books on PPT will show you how. But, as always, be sure you have the required permissions and cite your sources.

E. Adding Motion

1. PPT 2000 comes with two types of motion immediately available: **animation** of text and images on a slide, and short **motion clips** you may insert from a gallery.

2. To animate text and/or images on a PPT slide → Slide Show → Custom Animation. When the Custom Animation Window appears (see below) you may separately animate each slide object listed and checked in the upper left box. Once you have highlighted a slide object, activate the **Effects** tab by clicking on it. Proceed to the two boxes immediately below where you may select from a number of alternatives (**Fly - From Left** is used in this example) and, after making your selection, click OK. Now go on to the other objects on this slide you wish to animate, highlight each in turn, and repeat the process. When you are finished, you may review your work by clicking on Preview.

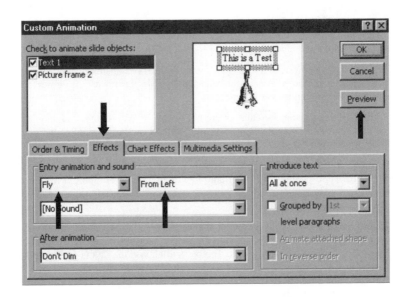

3. PPT 2000 also has a number of Motion Clips you may place on your slides. To access this option → Insert → Movies and Sounds → Movie From Galley. Proceed as you did for images to select and insert your desired clip. Once on your slide, the clip is treated like any other object and may be animated. It will play automatically when it appears on the slide.

4. Longer video clips are available on CD from commercial sources. Check publications such as *Multimedia World* and *Multimedia Online* for clip collections that are already in a digitized format you can import to PPT (AVI and MPEG are two popular formats). To truly personalize your presentation with your own video, you must digitize it using special equipment and techniques beyond the scope of this booklet. But once in a compatible digital format, the video is inserted by → Insert → Movies and Sounds → Movie from File → Insert Clip.

IMPORTANT: Once you have finished with your first slide, you move on to a new slide by → Insert → New Slide, and that will take you back to the AutoLayout window.

5. Hyperlinking to a movie may be a better option, if you encounter difficulty inserting the movie (Windows users with QuickTime on their systems may encounter this problem). Move to the slide where you want to link to the movie file, choose Slide Show → Action Buttons → Movie (or the icon that looks like a movie camera). Click and drag on the slide to create a green movie button of any size. Choose "Hyperlink to:" and select "Other File . . ." Find and select your movie file, then select "Use relative path for hyperlink." Click **OK** and save. When in presentation mode, you can play this movie by clicking the green button—this will bring up the movie in the movie viewer set up on your system.

F. Working in the Slide Sorter View

1. While you are creating your presentation, you will be working in the Normal View most of the time. This View shows one slide at a time, which is perfect for adding, deleting and editing content. The limitation of the Normal View is that you can't see all the slides that make up your presentation. This is where the Slide Sorter View is invaluable. The Slide Sorter View works on the same principle as a light table used for 35mm slides. It allows you to inspect all the slides in your presentation, and then sort them into a sequence that you feel will work best for your lecture.

2. To get to the Slide Sorter View, go to View → Slide Sorter or simply click on the Slide Sorter button (it looks like a four-pane window) in the lower left corner of your Normal View screen (see next page).

3. If all the slides in your presentation are not visible on one screen, you may increase the number visible by going to the drop-down box on the far right of the Standard Toolbar and reducing the % number (66% in the example).

4. If you would like to **rearrange the sequence of your slides**, you may do so by clicking on the slide you wish to move and then dragging and dropping it to where you would like it (hold down the left mouse button, move the slide to its new location, and release the mouse button).

5. **To add a new slide** to your presentation click between the two slides where you want your new slide to be inserted. A long, vertical cursor will mark the spot. Click the **New Slide button** on the Standard Toolbar and choose the layout you want for the slide. The new slide will be added at the cursor. Double click on the new slide to move it to the Normal View for editing.

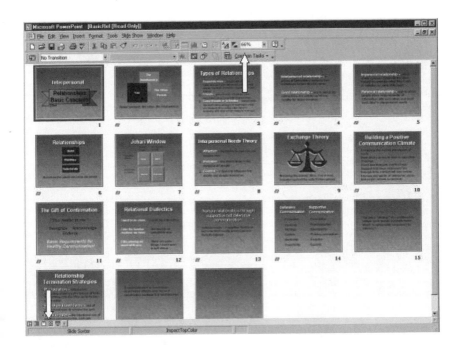

6. **To duplicate a slide**, click the slide you want to duplicate, then → Edit → Duplicate (or Ctrl+D). The duplicate slide is inserted immediately to the right of the original slide. This slide can now be moved to wherever in the presentation you would like it placed.

7. **To delete a slide**, click the slide and press Backspace or Delete on the keyboard. To retrieve a deleted slide → Edit → Undo or the back arrow on the Standard Toolbar.

8. **To add a slide from another presentation**, click between the two slides where you want your new slide to be inserted. The long, vertical cursor will mark the spot. Switch to the other presentation and click the slide you want to copy. Copy the selected slide by → Edit → Copy. Return to your original presentation and → Edit → Paste. The copied slide will be added at the spot you selected.

G. Saving Your Presentation

After creating your presentation or lecture, you will want to save your work by using one of the following methods:

1. Click the Save button (looks like a floppy disk) on the Standard toolbar. Choose the File → Save command from the Main Menu or Press Ctrl+S.

2. The first time you save, the **Save As** dialog box (see next page) appears for you to type in the name of your newly created file. In addition to selecting a filename, you must choose a folder into which you will place your file. My Document is a popular folder for saving on your computer's hard drive. Other saving site options are on a floppy disk (usually A drive), or for larger files a Zip disk or a CD. Your college's Instructional Technologies Department will have the expertise and often the hardware to help you save big files on Zips or CDs.

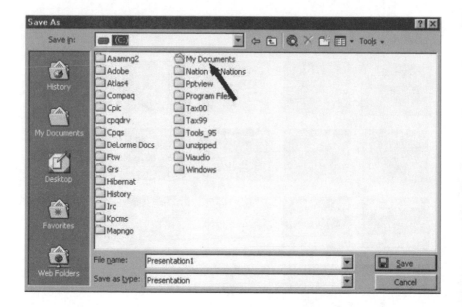

3. Save often. If you close your file or exit PPT without saving your presentation, consider it gone forever. Saving often also buys you insurance against losing everything in the event of a power interruption or a computer crash.

IV. Tailoring the MM CD for Your Lectures

Once you have mastered the basics of creating a PPT presentation, you have the ability to modify the presentations provided on the MM CD. One way is to follow these steps.

A. Moving a Presentation from the CD to Your Hard Drive

1. Place the MM CD in the CD drive.

2. Double click on the My Computer icon on your Windows Desktop, which will open a window that displays the drives on your computer.

3. Double click on the CD drive (should be your MM CD name preceding the drive letter), which will produce a window showing the files on your MM CD (see the example opposite, at top).

4. Drag and drop to your Windows Desktop the PPT presentation you wish to edit.

   Note: If you wish to keep any videos that are linked to this PPT presentation with it, you should also drag and drop these video files to your desktop at this time. Use the Slide by Slide Index at the back of this booklet to identify linked videos in a particular presentation. Next, return to the list of files on your MM CD and find the video camera icon with an abbreviated title that matches your linked video. Move it to the desktop.

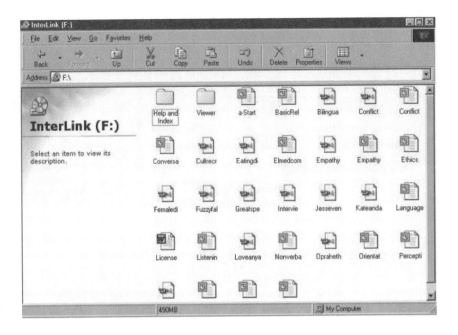

B. Modifying the Selected Presentation

1. Double click the PPT presentation you moved from your MM CD to your Windows Desktop. This will open up that presentation in PowerPoint.

2. Using the Normal and/or the Slide Sorter Views, make the changes that you want.

C. Saving Your Changes

1. After making your changes, save the modified version by clicking on the Save icon on the Standard Toolbar or → File → Save. A window like the one below will appear indicating that your file is "read-only." To save your modified version, click Yes and rename (in this example you might want to call the new version BasicRel2.ppt).

2. Besides renaming this file, you will also be asked where you would like to save it. If the files are small you may save then to a 3.5 floppy disk. However, your MM CD presentations are too large to save on a floppy. If you plan to use the same computer to play the new presentation as the one on which you created it, save your file to a

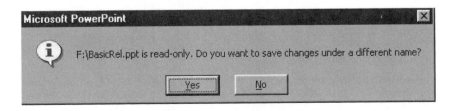

folder on your hard drive such as My Documents. If you plan to play your presentation on a different computer, then you must save on a transportable disk such as a Zip or a CD. Experience indicates that saving on a CD is preferable to a Zip for smooth swift presentation. If there is a linked video that is a part of the presentation, saving on a CD is a must because the video will play in a very jerky fashion on a Zip. Also remember that the linked video file(s) must also be saved with the modified version of the presentation on the same CD if it is going to be played on other computers.

V. Showing Your Presentation to Students

A. On a Classroom Computer

1. Sections II. A. and B. of this booklet take you through the basic steps for presenting a PPT lecture in your classroom. However, there are some additional tips that you may find helpful as you go along.

2. There may come the day when you will be asked to show your presentation without the aid of your personal computer. If you discover that the computer on which you will show your presentation meets all the Link system requirements but does not have PPT installed, don't panic. Your MM CD comes with a PPT Viewer for your use. To place the viewer on the computer you will be using follow these directions: with the MM CD in its drive, use My Computer to navigate to the **OPEN** screen and double click on the folder labeled Viewer (see section II. A. 5). When the file entitled Ppview__ appears, double click on it and follow the on-screen directions to install the viewer.

3. If you plan on using your own modified version of a MM CD lecture that you have transferred to your own Zip disk or CD and will not be using your own computer for your presentation, include the PPT Viewer that is on your MM CD when you create you own Zip/CD. This is done by dragging and dropping the Viewer File off the MM CD just as you drag and drop linked video clips.

4. When playing a video clip as part of your presentation: First, be patient when you come to the link slide. The clip will take some seconds to load before it automatically begins to play. Additional clicking of the mouse button while the clip loads instead of waiting patiently will throw the presentation off. Second, if you wish to **pause the video** during the course of play, one left click with the cursor in the picture portion of the video will pause the action. Another left click on the picture will **resume play**. Third, when you come to the end of the clip, or if you want to end the clip before the normal end of play, one left click with the cursor off the picture ends the video clip and takes you to the next PPT slide.

5. While making a PPT presentation, if you wish to **return to the previous view**, simply press the backspace key. This will take you back one step (either to the preceding object on the same slide or the previous slide).

6. During a PPT presentation, you may want to employ a **blank screen** to preclude distraction while talking or performing another activity. To generate a blank screen in the course of a PPT presentation, simply press **B** on your keyboard. To return to the PPT slide, press B again.

7. A final tip to keep in mind as you prepare your PPT presentation is to create a **final slide** for your show that has the standard background but is otherwise blank. You will then have a visual cue that you have come to the end.

B. In Print: Handouts and Transparencies

1. Audiences are often grateful for copies of the slides you present during your lecture. To print audience handouts, open your PPT presentation → File → Print on the standard menu bar. Using the **Print What** drop-down list, select **Handouts** with two, three, or six slides per page. The three slides per page provides enough space next to the images of the slides for the user to jot down notes. Check the **Grayscale** box and click **OK** to start printing.

    Caution: Providing these slide handouts to students may reduce note-taking.

2. In the event that you need transparencies with which to make your presentation, PPT will guide you in their production. Before you begin, make sure that you have the correct type of transparency acetate for the kind of printer you will be using in production. You **must** use Ink Jet acetate for Ink Jet printers and Laser acetate for Laser printers, otherwise the printer will malfunction. The packaging in which the transparency acetate comes will guide you in how to load it into your printer. Once these steps are taken, with your PPT presentation open, → File → Page Setup. In the **Page Setup** dialog box (above) select **Overhead** in the "Slides Sized For" drop-down list;

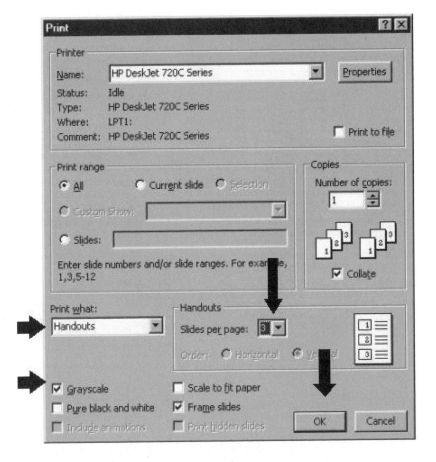

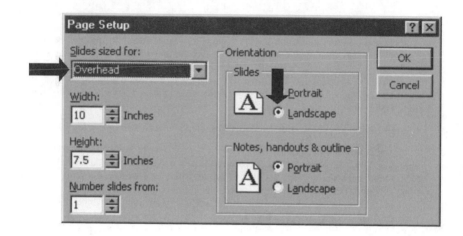

in the "Orientation Slides" section select the **Landscape** option; Click **OK** and go to File → Print → Current Slide and OK. If you do not select Current Slide your entire presentation will print.

Note: You may also produce transparencies by first making paper copies of your PPT slides and then with the correct type of transparency acetate for a copy machine, produce your overheads that way.

In all cases where you are using transparency acetate **do not touch** the prints until they are completely dry to avoid smudges.

C. On the Internet

1. PPT allows you to put your presentations on the Internet without needing to learn the special Web code known as HTML. A word or two of caution: when considering placing your presentations on the electronic superhighway, recognize that it may have a negative effect on class attendance and note-taking in class if you are also using the traditional instructional approach to reach your students. Also please note that the CNN video clips on your MM CD **may not be posted**, even on your Campus Web site. The CNN videos are for classroom use only.

2. If you have decided to publish your presentations on the Internet, PPT has a "wizard" that will lead you through converting your lecture slides to HTML. More advanced books cover this conversion process, and you will probably have to rely on the college's Web Director for assistance, but the process is not difficult.